Jersey
Hudson River Waterfront

Book two: LV, CNJ, Erie, DL&W and EL

(1941-1964)

Charles Caldes

edited by
Gary Coolick, John Hanson
and **Diane Bizub**

digital layout by
**Benjamin L. Bernhart,
Outer station Project**

Journal Square Publishing
701 Kingsland Avenue, Ridgefield, NJ 07657
ISBN 0-9760714-6-0
Copyright © 2010

Table of Contents

Acknowledgements. iv

The Lehigh Valley Railroad. 1

The Companies. 24

The Central Railroad of New Jersey. . . 34

The Erie, DL&W and EL Railroads. . . 59

Acknowledgments

Many thanks to Cynthia Harris and the staff of the Jersey City Library's New Jersey Room. Thanks to Ralph A Heiss for the use of his maps and charts. Thanks go to Gary Coolick of the Loose Caboose, John Hansen, Diane Bizub for their editing. Special thanks go to Benjamin Bernhart for his digital layout design of this book.

All photos are from the New jersey Rooms collection of the Jersey City Free Public Library unless otherwise noted.

The Lehigh Valley Railroad

At the edge of Pier B, one of the Lehigh Valley Railroad's many service Lighters is parked with its crew prepping for departure. 1954

The Lehigh Valley Railroad began with the incorporation in Pennsylvania of the Delaware, Lehigh, Schuylkill & Susquehanna Railroad on April 21, 1846. Seven years later the name was simplified to the Lehigh Valley Railroad. The Lehigh Valley Railroad would expand over the next few decades, eventually building a freight terminal in Jersey City in 1889 on land purchased adjoining the Morris Canal. Initially, the Lehigh Valley Railroad had leased the Morris Canal, including the Basin. It was clear that this property was of no use in its then present form, but would be ideal as a railhead where land met water. The Lehigh Valley went a step further and bought it outright, thus becoming a true presence on the Jersey City waterfront. The next expansion was in 1900 when the National Docks were purchased, giving the Lehigh Valley a significant parcel along the Hudson River. This was a necessity to compete with the other railroads as the region's prosperity grew. In 1923 the Lehigh Valley built the Claremont Terminal in southern Jersey City, a deep water port to handle ocean going vessels. Though modestly successful, the grandiose dreams of the railroad executives never materialized.

The Lehigh Valley was quick to see that the steam engine was not going to be the only method of moving freight and people around. In 1945

Pier B was a servicing structure keeping the Lehigh Valley's water craft running. 1954

the famed FT cowl units appeared on its roster. Steam would be gone by 1951 which coincided with the company's lack of profits. The 1950's would begin the slide downward as rail shipments started to steadily decline. The post war climate was of a new nature. Business was no longer done as before. The truck and the airplane were pulling out their share of the transport pile in bigger fistfuls each year. The problem for the Lehigh Valley was that they just did not have enough traffic to keep on going at the pace they were geared up for. They were in the wrong place at the wrong time. As the overall picture for the railroads throughout the industry became harsher, many corporate moves were to be made, most in desperation. In 1962 the Pennsylvania Railroad purchased the Lehigh Valley. But this did neither any good. The descent was in 4th gear and nothing was going to stop the disaster that would take down all of the region's railroads. On June 24, 1970 the Lehigh Valley Railroad would declare bankruptcy three days after the Pennsylvania Railroad, now the Penn Central, had done so. For twenty five years the Lehigh Valley Railroad fought a good fight, never giving up to the end. On April 1st, 1976, the Lehigh Valley Railroad and the rest of Jersey City's waterfront railroads threw in the towel and were absorbed into Conrail.

The Lehigh Valley's double set of Transfer Bridges stood out among the nearest waterfront structures. A tug is about to nudge a car float out into the Hudson as soon as a few more box cars are placed. Note the Ferry to the left. 1954.

This 1941 photo shows in detail the beautiful lines of this simple wooden Lehigh Valley Pontoon Bridge.

Pier C, like the rest of the LV's piers was slanted to the east. The Tide Basin was of limited width. With angled piers there was more room for maneuvering water traffic. The design also allowed a higher number of tracks to enter and work the piers. The norm back in the 1950's for the riverfront railroads was to own and moor many lighters and to use them as needed. The way business was done 60 years ago wouldn't fit into the corporate philosophies of today.

Tidewater Basin

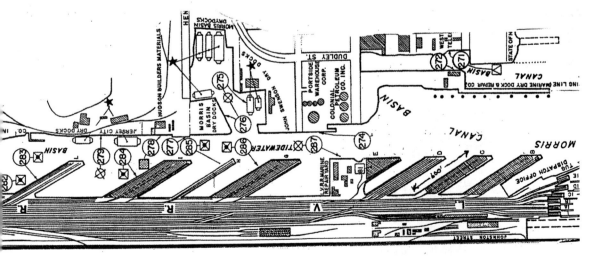

A tug approaches LV's Lighter No.66 at the edge of pier D, which is filled with rows of box cars. It must have been enjoyable working for the Lehigh Valley back then. The constant movements of trains and water craft, though dangerous, were reminders every day that tasks of substance were being performed. Every LV man and woman at the end of the week could look at their paycheck and feel a sense of pride at a job well done. 1954.

A lone hopper has been set out on Pier D's west track. The pier's single car unloading device was a braced structure with an overhang to accommodate a pulley system attached to a funnel to handle grain etc. To the right was Pier E.

Pier F had a little of everything on it. In view were pilings, lumber and barrels neatly placed around the grouping of single story buildings. The trucks in the photo are terrific examples of the vehicles of that era. 1954

The Lehigh Valley Railroad's three sets of pontoon bridges are resting in empty mode, which was becoming more and more a common sight as the 1950's progressed. To the left are the twin Lift Bridges with their famous Lehigh Valley lettering spread proudly across them. Note the tower at the far right. 1954

The LV's tiny two track pier was nestled between Pier G & Pier 1. It's neat how the planners way back then had the foresight to include this minimal piece of extended land. Over the years this tiny pier would carry an exaggerated amount of tonnage. 1954

Pier L's five tracks were used mostly for the off loading of freight that only Gondoliers could carry to the waiting Stick Lighters. Check out the heavy duty Gantry Crane, rail bridges and the high rise tower topped with flood lights to facilitate night movements. Railroading was and is a 24 hour operation. The Lehigh Valley Railroad didn't bother with end bumpers on all the tracks on pier L, they just placed old ties at the ends of four of them. 1954

A Lighter with a bunch of high standing crates waits for its turn to help fill the cargo hull of a hungry freighter.

Annual Railroad Freight Moved by the Lehigh Valley Railroad in Jersey City, New Jersey

Year	Total Annual Freight	Local Freight
1959	1,843,675	361,368
1958	2,175,400	337,575
1957	2,507,022	403,531
1956	2,733,650	493,925
1955	2,793,563	433,125
1954	2,544,625	386,946
1953	2,806,277	485,933
1952	2,875,221	411,808
1951	4,236,664	528,799
1950	2,875,172	426,423
1949	3,153,833	419,763
1940	2,961,366	1,578
1939	2,511,836	616

Source: Port of New York Authority, Port Development Department

The Jersey City waterfront was still hopping during the height of the Great Depression. The construction work being done at the end of the Lehigh Valley Railroad Milk Platform may not have been a major job, but it was extensive enough to warrant temporary track to be laid to allow a rail crane to take care of the heavy lifting. Henderson & Essex Streets. 1930's

Above: The Lehigh Valley in 1954 had already begun to give in to the ever quickening shift away from the once bustling Hudson River traffic to other ports and modes of transportation. Though there are plenty of cars parked in view, there are also a goodly number of watercraft that are never going back into action. The decline of a once great industry is never a happy sight. **Below:** When looking beyond the moored Cleary Brothers barge on the Basin, a wonderment of the past is evident: cranes, smoke stacks, oil tanks, water tanks, buildings of all types and the Colgate Clock. This is what one gazed at from an eye level perspective. June 2, 1950

The shores of the Morris Canal Basin were filled with lumber and other materials that accumulated over the years. The area is cleaner, neater and modernized now, but there was something special about all those beams and masts that you couldn't miss noticing that are now long gone. June 2, 1950

STATIONS FOR RECEIPT AND DELIVERY OF FREIGHT—Continued
(For List of Prohibited and Restricted Articles at These Stations, see Items 1600 to 1750.)

Item		LEHIGH VALLEY RAILROAD
550	Name of Station	Jersey City (Grand St.), N. J.
	Location	Grand St., Jersey City, N. J.
	Facilities	Team track facilities and freight house facilities. Electric traveling crane—capacity 30 tons. Electric crawler type crane with 56 inch magnet. Covered automobile unloading platform. End door unloading facilities.
	Deliveries	Carload and less than carload freight.
	Application of Rates	New York Harbor rates apply, except where tariffs applying specify otherwise.
	Crane Charges	For charges for use of Cranes, refer to Rule A-202.
	Waybill Instructions	Waybill to Grand St., Jersey City, N. J.
		LEHIGH VALLEY RAILROAD
555	Name of Station	Jersey City (Johnson Ave.), N. J.
	Location	Johnson Ave., Jersey City, N. J.
	Facilities	Team track facilities.
	Deliveries	Carloads only.
	Application of Rates	New York Harbor rates apply, except where tariffs applying specify otherwise.
	Waybill Instructions	Waybill to Johnson Ave., Jersey City, N. J.

Claremont Terminal

The Claremont Terminal was built by the Lehigh Valley Railroad in 1923 with great expectations. It was located a couple of hundred feet north of the massive Pennsylvania Railroads Hudson river Greenville complex in southern Jersey City, the primary concept of the 149 acre terminal was to eliminate the need of lighters by creating a deep harbor port for sea going vessels to be serviced directly at the Lehigh Valley pier, which was 900 feet long by 136 feet wide. The Claremont Terminal pier would be able to handle multiple ships simultaneously, utilizing the pier's heavy duty cranes and equipment with a large feeding yard. The Terminal would bring a new efficiency to the Port of Jersey City. Though never reaching its envisioned greatness, the Claremont Terminal was a success for many years.

On this day in 1954 the Claremont Terminal appears to be jammed with water craft. The Lehigh Valley's pier was capable of handling multiple ocean going freighters and Lighters of all breeds. The terminal was a one stop express transfer station.

The Claremont Terminal was a big complex. Just the position of the warehouse sitting between two docked freighters at each end gives the impression of considerable length. Scrap metal Lighters somehow always seem at home on the Jersey City waterfront. Note the grouping of heavy duty cranes. 1950's

A line of Lighters waits alongside the terminal warehouse to take their turn off-loading a ship or cargo from the pier. It is easy to figure out that the Lehigh Valley had high hopes with so many duplexed bays the length of the structure. 1954

Map of Claremont Terminal

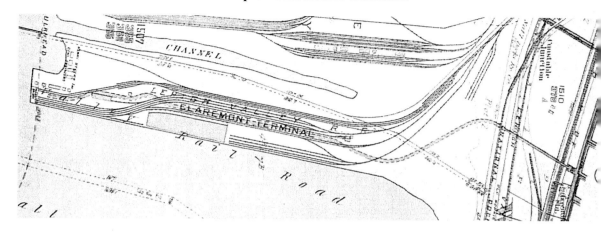

The view of the inshore end of the Claremont Terminal's pier shows a docked freighter with a group of Lighters moored at its side. The heavy duty cranes that did the loading and unloading of the ships would do the job as efficiently as possible for the times (1954), but to no avail, as the container ship was on the way and would take over the movement of sea going goods with a new era of productivity. The freighter was doomed in its present form.

Black Tom

Above: The National Docks Grain Elevator on Black Tom was a thirty-three silo operation that loaded lighters and barges directly from the structure. January 15, 1964 **Below:** The Lehigh Valley Grain Elevator is loading a Hold Barge at pier side. Check out the angle of the Hold Barge sitting in the water as it is being filled. January 15, 1964

The Lehigh Valley's Black Tom location was northeast of Claremont Yard and south of the CNJ's yards and structures. It actually was secluded from the rest of the Hudson River's many rail works. Looking at this photo it's hard to believe something so visually overwhelming was ever there. January, 1954

Not exactly a bright spot, the Lehigh Valley Railroad's five story Black Tom warehouse was old and had not been well maintained for years by time this photo was taken in the early 1950's.

Claremont Yard Leading Into Black Tom Island

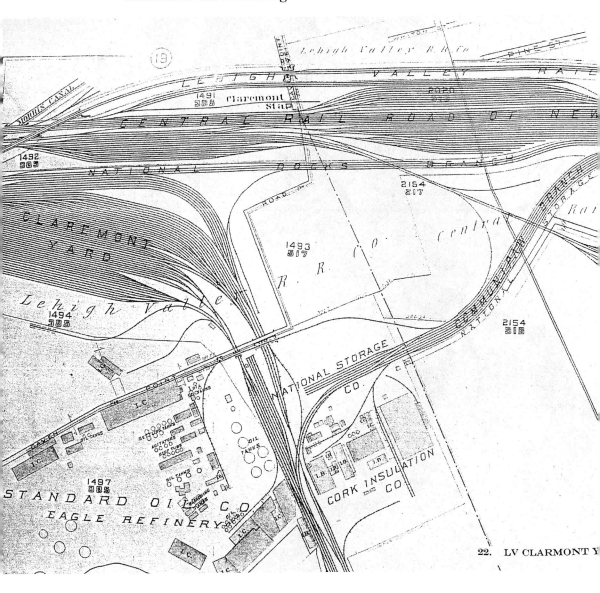

Black Tom is in busy mode this day in 1954. The waters are filled with Tugboats and all types of Lighters.

Black Tom Island

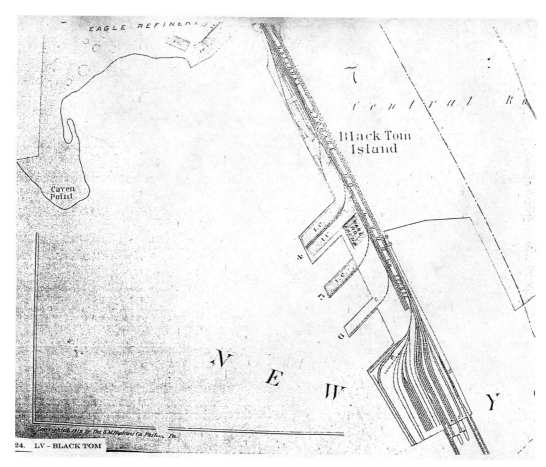

Looking southeast along the basin the many types of water bound visitors are apparent. All kinds of lighters and barges are moored to handle the movement of goods shipped by the Lehigh Valley Railroad. Strings of box cars, tank cars, gondolas, etc. wait to off-load or pick up freight. November 30, 1961

The LV's long thin waterfront yard efficiently hooked up with the angled piers and warehouses along the Morris Basin. Shown here are Piers E & F. Across the Basin is the Portside Terminal seen in 1961 with three white painted tanks. Note the rows of truck trailers.

The Lehigh Valley RR's Claremont Yard, looking east.

The Lehigh Valley's waterfront trackage was by far the smallest of all the Hudson River railroads in Jersey City. Though barely a dozen plus tracks wide, the yard was not only laid out for maximum productivity, but was a joy to look at. There was a certain symmetrical uniqueness to it that no other rail head in the port had. The lines of its trackage almost appear to have been laid out by a team of engineer / artists. Note the diverse buildings and equipment that covered the piers. 1954.

The Companies

The Morris Dry Dock was located along the northern side of the Tide basin. The nearby location of repair / maintenance companies like this made it easier and quicker for the railroads to get their equipment back into service. During WWII the dry docks must have worked day and night. 1950's

The Jersey City Floating Dry Dock Company is seen here working on the Virginia. Back in the 1950'S the railroads were still utilizing singular types of equipment such as this Lighter used for transporting livestock. Note the Pennsylvania Railroad covered barge. 1954

The Lehigh Valley Railroad Lighter No.14 is moored at the piers of the Hudson Building & Morris Dry Dock companies. This eastern view gives a good idea of the New York skyline of the mid 1950s.

Four cranes are working the scrap yard located on the Northen side of the Tide Basin on this day in 1954. The Woody Wagon and the boats stand out among the piles of discarded junk spread out in separate groupings. Note the water tower at the left.

FLOAT SCHEDULES

NEW YORK HARBOR

PIERS	EASTBOUND		WESTBOUND	
	Leave Jersey City	Arrive New York	Leave New York	Arrive Jersey City
Pier 8, North River	4.45A 5.00A 7.30A	5.00A 5.15A 7.45A	5.15P 7.15P 7.30P	5.30P 7.30P 7.45P
Pier 38, North River	2.00A 3.00A 3.30A 4.00A 7.00A	2.30A 3.30A 4.00A 4.30A 7.45A	5.30P 6.00P	6.00P 6.30P ....
Pier 66, North River	5.15A 8.15A	6.00A 9.00A	5.30P	6.15P .....
West 27th St. Yard, North River	6.00A 12.15P	6.45A 1.00P	5.00P	5.45P .....
Pier 44, East River	1.00A	2.00A	3.45P	4.45P
48th St., East River	4.00A 6.00A	5.00A 7.00A	4.00P	5.15P .....
125th St., East River	3.30A	4.45A	3.30P	5.00P
149th St., East River (Bronx Terminal)	3.30A 11.30A	5.00A 1.00P	3.00P	5.00P .....

    Lehigh Valley R.R. also operates floats to and from Long Island R.R. at Long Island City, and NYC at 60th St. (68th St.).

    NYNH&H R.R. operates floats between Oak Point and Jersey City.

    B.E.D. Terminal, Bush Dock, Jay Street and New York Dock Co. operate floats between Brooklyn and Jersey City.

The eastern view of the Bay Oil bulk Head was a depot filled with pilings and simple wooden goods of all sizes and shapes. 1954

The Open Fingers pier looking into Jersey City has a line of Lighters moored alongside a pair of Hold Barges.

Bay Oils Third Finger Piers were topped with this considerable warehouse. 1954

Jersey City's Portside Terminal consisted of a group of oil tanks flanked by concrete walls. It was not a mega player in New Jersey's oil industry, but was considered big for such a confined area. 1954

A close up of the Tide Water Basins Portside Terminal shows the hundreds of 55 gallon drums stacked or scattered around the grounds. Note the competing gasoline company signs ready to fill up the next thirsty boat to moor. The structure of the bulkhead was constructed to last and handle a lot of abuse to protect the tanks. This contrasts with the shape of most of the Hudson River piers, which at this point (1950's) were not receiving the kind of upkeep they needed.

Located at the foot of Jersey Avenue (1 Jersey Avenue) smack in the middle of the CNJ and LV properties was the Schiavone - Bonomo Scrap Yard. Begun in 1899, the firm grew with the region and the times, becoming a major importer and exporter of scrap. The need for metals of all types was growing in demand as the prosperity of the 20th Century expanded along with the country's population. Recycling is not a new concept; Schiavone - Bonomo was handling 75,000 tons annually of ferrous & non-ferrous scrap right through the 1960's. For many years they accounted for nearly half of the Metro area's scrap tonnage. 1954

ALL RAILROADS - ANNUAL MERCHANDISE LIGHTERAGE

Year	Total Merchandise Lighterage	True Lighterage	Rail to Keel Truck to Keel
1960	4,046,984	3,222,317	824,667
1959	3,876,381	3,142,014	734,367
1958	4,670,813	3,838,563	832,250
1957	5,686,245	4,660,551	1,025,694
1956	6,049,169	4,910,539	1,138,630
1955	5,880,807	4,716,311	1,164,496
1954	5,282,887	4,419,164	863,723
1953	6,125,460	5,130,417	995,043
1952	6,889,760	6,022,809	866,951
1951	7,063,838	6,122,485	941,353
1950	5,960,227	5,212,415	747,812
1949	6,954,421	6,182,188	772,233
1940	7,415,370	6,922,029	493,341
1939	5,304,265	4,916,862	387,403

(Figures are in Short Tons)

ALL RAILROADS - ANNUAL RAILROAD FREIGHT, JERSEY CITY WATERF

Year	Total Annual Freight	Local Freight	Tidewater Coal	Grain Lighterage	Merchandise Lighterage
1960	- -	- -	5,618,535	71,450	3,547,775
1959	18,119,361	2,628,333	4,849,000	91,692	3,460,712
1958	19,632,968	2,693,445	5,795,947	153,223	4,069,721
1957	21,998,728	3,363,239	5,689,050	133,642	5,018,141
1956	25,003,314	3,604,926	7,166,989	350,524	5,331,952
1955	23,486,486	3,680,152	5,678,400	302,085	5,197,089
1954	22,040,951	3,480,407	5,522,926	235,699	4,768,983
1953	24,279,036	3,654,324	5,806,530	339,589	5,310,324
1952	26,798,909	4,865,676	6,522,419	112,284	5,973,426
1951	27,854,983	3,688,029	7,269,002	287,902	6,027,654
1950	25,760,590	4,227,210	6,440,673	239,736	5,081,678
1949	24,663,858	3,539,560	5,528,133	421,160	5,947,195
1940	24,845,180	2,897,584	6,964,324	178,753	6,252,542
1939	22,282,634	2,233,284	7,231,407	285,670	4,667,420

*Includes Railroad to railroad local freight destined for delivery in the Port District (exc City local freight) as well as railroad to railroad movements through the Port District.

Source: Port of New York Authority, Port Development Department

The Central Railroad of New Jersey

The Johnson Avenue Yard was still packed with rolling stock of all types in 1958. The Hudson River was drawing less freight each year but would for another decade present a picture of continuing commerce that wasn't ready to quit. The Jersey City waterfront was a flat man made extension into the river that was most suitable for the efficient movement of freight cars. The switchers the CNJ employed were light weights of low horse power easily pulling strings of box cars, etc. all day long. I like the way the ties appear to have sunken and blended into the fill. It must have been a sight to have seen such a massively wide grouping of yards running for miles. Taken for granted back then by everyone, now gone and replaced by miles of high rises.

Communipaw Yard

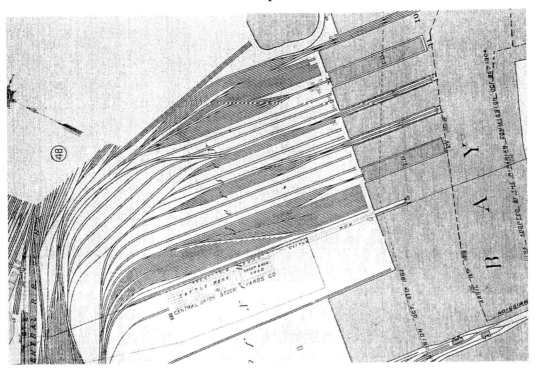

The Central Railroad of New Jersey was more than an icon on the Hudson River waterfront. To those who were passengers or employees, the CNJ was an institution like no other in their lives. Jersey City's place in the world was connected to the growth and prosperity of the CNJ. The importance of the CNJ in Jersey City began in 1864 when the CNJ completed its main line across Newark Bay. Ferry service from the new Terminal at Communipaw Avenue now fed from commuter trains, and an explosively growing freight presence would lead to a lucrative waterfront business for the CNJ. Along with the other nearby railroads, Jersey City had become a place to dwell in; close, but not too close to all the jobs in New York City.

The CNJ remained prosperous into the 1930's, but went the way of so many other once healthy corporations. The Great Depression took its toll on the CNJ. The lack of freight would place it in receivership (1939-1949). The damage was done and the CNJ would never fully recover over the next 27 years. In 1972 they pulled out of Pennsylvania and shifted the bulk of their Freight operations to Port Elizabeth. The Aldene Plan in 1967 had already finished off passenger service in Jersey City. The only thing left was to go the route of Federal absorption via Conrail in 1976. All good things must come to an end.

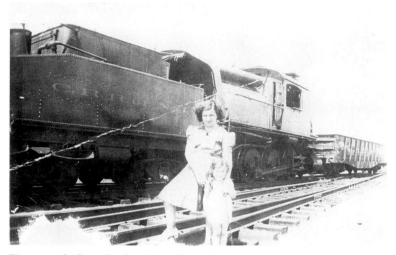

Dressed in their Sunday best, Mr. Mclaughlin's daughters Rosemary and Joann smile for the camera, next to the tender of a CNJ camelback engine. 1940 Courtesy Victor J Urban Jr.

Mr. McLaughlin (standing on the ground) poses with a buddy in this 1940's photo. Mr. Mclaughlin switched the CNJ car floats for many years. It must have been a relief when they changed over from steam to diesel power. Switching cars via steam was a laborious job. The ease of the new diesel powered engines would have allowed for many less aches and pains. Courtesy Victor J. Urban Jr.

As a diesel switcher works one of the Communipaw Yards piers, the New York City skyline creates a stark contrast to the base work area of the Jersey City waterfront. 1960's

Pier 7 tended to get congested as seen from the water at the outer end. This section of the CNJ's Hudson River Waterfront property was capable of docking vessels of considerable tonnage. On this day in 1954, the Maria Polina G has a pair of Weeks Stev Co. cranes planted on heavy duty barges, transferring cargo. Before containerization monopolized the Nation's ports, the floating crane was a very efficient way to handle the difficult logistics of loading and unloading large hulled ships. There are many large cranes, other vessels, a barge laden with scrap metal and a small boat at dockside, giving the reader a feel for an ordinary day's activities, on the Jersey City's waterfront.

Pier 14 had a full length warehouse with trackage running along side its southern exposure. It was so much more enjoyable back when there were so many railroad companies all with individual boxcars. One could never tire of seeing the different corporate icons proudly painted on each piece of rolling stock. Then you could pick out on any one track, on any day, on the Jersey city waterfront more cars from more railroads than exist today. 1954

CENTRAL NEW JERSEY RAILROAD - ANNUAL RAILROAD FREIGHT, JERSEY CITY

Year	Total Annual Freight	Local Freight	Tidewater Coal	Grain Lighterage	Merchandise Lighterage
1960	- -	- -	3,696,198	- -	873,021
1959	6,504,301	466,512	3,228,675	- -	883,867
1958	7,086,061	447,299	3,850,158	- -	970,931
1957	7,674,648	583,351	3,965,826	- -	1,051,713
1956	9,035,705	640,602	5,045,103	- -	1,149,640
1955	7,873,998	577,768	3,925,130	- -	1,127,027
1954	7,897,151	593,192	4,157,485	- -	1,016,182
1953	8,540,281	662,877	4,369,088	- -	1,148,421
1952	8,979,482	659,217	4,705,588	- -	1,131,759
1951	9,935,606	799,167	5,364,534	- -	1,115,338
1950	8,873,283	756,748	4,348,152	- -	1,093,989
1949	7,750,871	738,840	3,513,442	- -	1,054,096
1940	8,208,684	773,538	4,014,986	- -	1,277,316
1939	7,500,315	766,830	3,772,902	- -	1,045,474

*Includes B & O Lighterage from CRR piers.

Source: Port of New York Authority, Port Development Department

This photo was taken from the Pennsylvania Railraod tug Lancaster on May 9th, 1941, seven months before World War II would start. Once war came, the CNJ and its sister railroads would pounce into a never before controlled frenzy of transporting the supplies needed to the factories and the finished products to our troops to battle the enemy. The location is the south side of the CNJ float Bridges. When you see a scene like this you have to marvel at how comely the brakemen ride the bumping, bouncing boxcars as if they were out taking in the beauty of the Hudson River.

Just south of the CNJ passenger Terminal a car float with hoppers and boxcars waits to begin its short run across the lower Hudson to the New York side. A tug and a grouping of Derrick lighters complete the view westward. 1954

Resting between Piers 11 & 13 is a mix of lighters, Stick lighters and Derrick lighters waiting for the call to get shoved out and toil aside their next assigned vessel. 1954

In 1954 when this photo was taken, the CNJ had already begun its financial descent. The warehouse that comprised Pier 5 was well into a state of disrepair. Planks are loose or missing, doors are ajar and the vandals have just started their favorite pastime of smashing windows. Yet the CRR of NJ lettering still is going to give a vivid impression as to which railroad owned the pier to those passing by on the Hudson.

The McMyler Dumper

The McMyler Dumper was one big powerful piece of machinery. "Big Mac," as it was known, was built right after World War I, which ended in 1918. The McMyler Dumper was Located at the southern end of the CNJ's property astride the 900 foot Pier 18. At 90 feet tall, Big Mac stood out among Jersey City's many diverse Hudson River waterfront structures.

The McMyler Dumper had only one purpose and that was to unload the contents of hopper cars into the hulls of ships and barges. Big Mac did this by grabbing hold of a hopper that was placed in position by an Iron Mule and simply rotated it until the coal slid into the pan of a telescoping delivery chute that in turn would deposit the contents into a waiting hull. This could be repeated every 50 seconds. Up to 80 Hull Barges would be in the immediate area waiting their turn to be filled. Normally 20 - 25 cars per hour were handled. This pace was found to be the most efficient tonnage to run. The two separate dumper machines usually averaged 20 -22 barges a day between them, but could do much more when needed.

The dumpers were run 20 hours daily with two - eight man crews. The yards added another dozen per shift. The coal cars were classified as either Anthracite and placed in the A yard or Bituminous, which would wind up in the B yard. During the winter, when things slowed down, only one dumper would be in use while the other was maintained and overhauled.

The B&O, Reading and the Western Maryland corporate emblems were the most frequently noticed in the CNJ's large yard leading up to Pier 18. Surprisingly, none of the 1,000,000 or so cars over the years ended up in the Hudson. Murphy's law never kicked in. But the hulls of a few barges gave out once in a while and sank at pier side.

Leading up to the Dumper were two thawing sheds producing temperatures exceeding 150 degrees. To power these buildings and the rest of the high energy consumption operation, 1.5 - 3 carloads of coal were used up daily.

Never considered to be of modern design, the McMyler Dumper was one of the east coast's busiest loaders. The New York Harbor was the right place to be due to New England's growing demands for coal. Big

Mac turned out to be a great investment for the CNJ. 25% of its revenue was derived from Pier 18 well into the 1950's. Seventy-two shippers were utilizing the Dumper with well over a hundred types of coal grade handled.

Big Mac's potential was proven during the massive industrial build up to World War II. In 1943 the dumpers worked around the clock doing over 19,000,000 tons of shore to ship delivery. That was almost 4 times more than a good year of peacetime movements. Big Mac accomplished much more than it was ever designed for. It was a proud time for the CNJ and its employees.

The usefulness of the McMyler Dumper and Pier 18 waned as Jersey City's waterfront suffered from the loss of one shipper after another. In the end it stood still and alone. Now not a single trace is left. It is as if it was never there.

Pier 18 -- Trackage around the McMyler Dumper

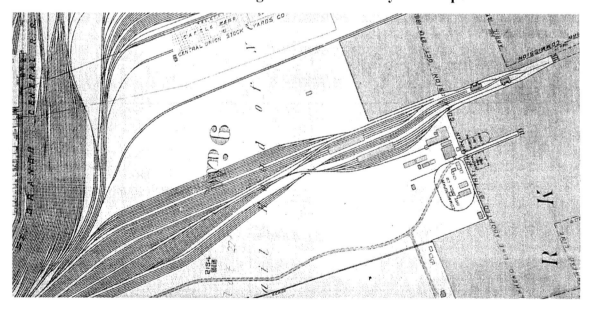

The area north of Pier18 was where the Hull Barges waited their turn to get loaded from the Big Mac Dumper.

A pair of Red Star Hull Barges are moored on the southern side of Pier 18. Barges like the No.75 were very common sights on the Hudson River. For many years a good portion of the fuel needs of the region were satisfied from pier 18's twin McMyler dumpers. The nearly constant loading of barges and the massive superstructures made one peering in this direction feel a sense of endless strength and continuity. 1959

This view of Pier 18 clearly shows the concrete supports for the elevated trackage that the Iron Mules would shove the coal hoppers up. They were built for the long term and stayed in action as a part of the load dumping operation for many decades. 1950's

Name	Acres	Land	Improvements
Greenville Yds. (PRR)	385	$12,200/a	$7,409,000
Claremont Term. (LVRR)	149	18,000/a	650,000
Block 1497 Lot 1 (CRRNJ)	- - -	- - -	- - -
Black Tom. Nat. Docks (LVRR)	37**	10,000/a	238,000
180 Acre Site (CRRNJ)	- -	- - -	- - -
22J Center (CRRNJ)	98	17,500/a	1,500,000
83 Acre Site (CRRNJ)	- -	- - -	- - -
Main Term. (CRRNJ)	191	26,675/a	3,343,000
Communipaw Yds. (LVRR)	53*	43,000/a	1,000,000
18 Acre Site (CRRNJ)	- -	- - -	- - -
Exchange Pl. (PRR)	10	- - -	- - -
Harborside (PRR)	- -	- - -	- - -
Harsimus (PRR)	125	52,000/a	1,800,000
J.C. Stockyards (PRR)	15	87,120/a	208,000
Pavonia Yds. (Erie RR)	85	52,000/a	2,700,000
Pier 9 (Erie RR)	- -	- - -	- - -
Lackawanna Yd. (LRR)	132	57,000/a	1,800,000
TOTALS	1,280 (24± underwater)	$36,588,725	$20,648,100

* Underwater
** Half Underwater

Top: Both dumpers are in use this day. The pier was set up for heavy use when necessary. Note the Ferry Boat in the background. **Middle:** Thousands of rivets went into the construction of the twin McMyler Dumpers. They did not last for a century but easily could have. A P&LE coal hopper is about to be lifted and its contents emptied into the hull of a barge. **Bottom:** The maintenance crews regularly had to scale the dumpers. At 90 feet in height, the cold steel of the machinery presented a daily struggle with gravity. The many beams, gears and cables that were moving parts worked 20 hour days and this amount of use caused wear and tear that had to be constantly repaired or replaced. Working on Pier 18 was a tough job which represented the norm for a city whose success was based on industry.

A B&O hopper is heading back to the level surface of the Johnston Avenue Yard. Soon the hopper will join a string of similar B&O hoppers and head back to the coal fields for another load.

A New York Central hopper slides past the control tower which was located on the southern edge of Pier 18. Working in view of the Statue of Liberty could never have become ordinary.

The single operator sits at a small console that would have been state of the art in 1952. Note the open windows. The CNJ, like so much of corporate America, had not yet realized the enhancements to productivity that AC created.

Top: Behind the NYC hopper the concrete abutments of the ramp can be clearly observed. With the tremendous pressure that years of the endless shifting of loaded coal hoppers created, the work track and its supports had to be built for the duration. **Middle**: The retarders were an important part of the pier's maximum efficiency concept. They simply fought gravity and allowed the empties to gradually slip back into the yard. **Bottom**: Pier 18's control tower was manned by a single employee. The operation was broken down to the basics of what had to be accomplished: get hoppers to the dumper as quickly and safely as possible, pick them up and unload the coal into a barge and get the empty hopper off the pier back into the Johnston Ave. Yard. How very cool looking was the control panel with all the advanced, for the day, dials and switches!

Above: These two photographs depict the Iron Mule in action. The Iron Mule ran under the rails of the pier on its own set of steel. Note the retarders. Illumination for night work performed by the crews was provided by rows of angled floodlights. **Below:** The approach from Johnston Yard onto Pier 18. Note the bumper track under the coaling tower.

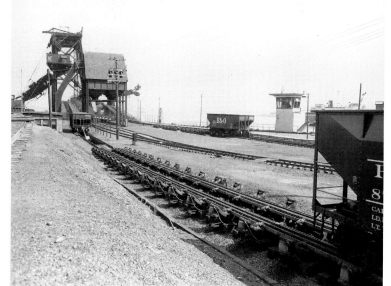

Top: Pier 18's track layout was set up for multiple hoppers to be in motion at one time. This was achieved with automatic turnouts and the Iron Mules all controlled and monitored by the pier's tower crewman. The Dumper on the left has its delivery chute in the lowered position while the southern dumper's chute is in the raised position.

Middle: This photo gives a ground level look at the center track turnout and the overhead lines that extended down most of the pier.

Another view of the Control tower.

All photographs on pages 48-53 are from the collection of the Outer Station Project.

This aerial shot shows the two entrances into the Central Railroad of New Jersey's Hudson River waterfront property. To the left the tracks lead to the Passenger Terminal with its massive protective shed. The entrance to the terminal was geared for the movement of multiple trains in and out at the same time. The passenger competition was intense and when a minute could be shaved off a schedule it meant something. To the right the freight traffic veered off into one of the CNJ's yards. A couple of hundred yards south of the two side by side signal towers, the turnouts for The Lehigh Valley's Black Tom Island and its Grain Elevator were located. Just north of the CNJ terminal the LV's other freight yard and piers were located, placing the much bigger CNJ smack in the middle. January 16, 1964

A CNJ caboose passes northward on the Belt Line as a couple of executives walk the tracks. Perhaps they were out of the office trying their best to get a feel of this once prosperous railroad that was entering deeper into a lessening state of commerce. It would take more than anything they could come up with that day or any other day. Times change and the CNJ didn't or couldn't. Early 1960's

Central Railroad of New Jersey Waterfront

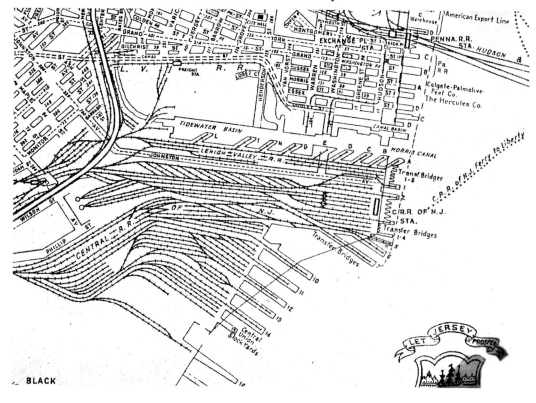

A CNJ cowl unit pulling freight on Belt Line 13 was a regular sight right into the 1960's. Working or living in one of the buildings near to the Beltway was a challenge to those who didn't appreciate the thick sounds and rumblings of thousands of tons of passing steel on steel at all times of the day and night. The portion of the Belt Line pictured here is elevated about half way up to the high point of Jersey City.

The CNJ Greenville Station was located a few hundred yards west of the river front. It stood out due to the long pedestrian overhead walkway over the trackage. There being so many tracks dividing Jersey City up into parcels, considerable walkways were a necessity when the rails ruled the transport business. When this photo was taken in 1954, the CNJ was already steadily losing ground. The end of World War II brought on a new middle class and with each new automobile purchased, one less rail passenger round trip ticket got stamped.

The Central Railroad of New Jersey was a multi yard major player in Jersey City. Its passenger terminal, Communipaw and Johnston Avenue Yards, and Pier 18 with its twin coal dumpers, took up much of the Hudson River water front. This aerial view from the mid 1960's shows the CNJ's position where river met bay. The action on the water is evident with so many ferry boats and tugs making their repetitive journeys. You can't tell what train is in motion but that was a constant on rails even as commerce had lessened in the region. It would take another decade before Conrail would take over this symmetrical tangle of curved trackage leading to the world's greatest river.

It's a few days after the Thanksgiving holiday of 1961 and the CNJ along with the LV properties look like they are doing a brisk business. The many passenger, mixed freight cars, barges and lighters give the visual feel of heavy action. The overview of this section of the Jersey City waterfront is filled with many different types of industrial structures. There are oil tanks, coal trestles, warehouses and factories spread out in what actually is a compact area. Note the snow topped ferry boats.

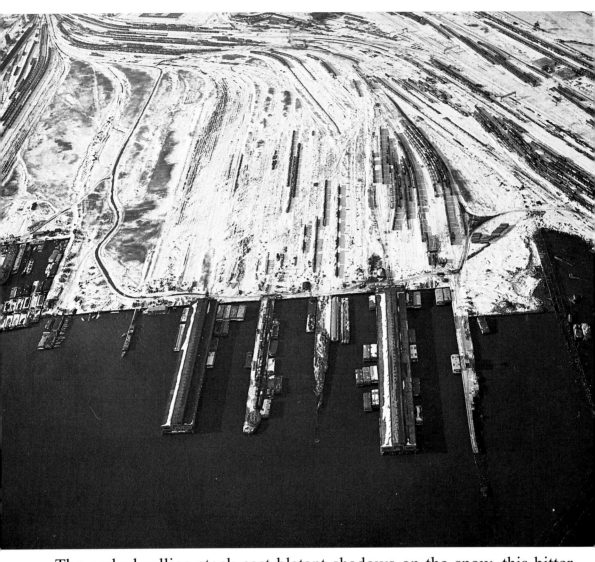

The parked rolling stock cast blatant shadows on the snow, this bitter cold mid day in January 1964, at the CNJ Communipaw yards. It must have been harsh working any of the Hudson's yards, especially the CNJ's being so wide and open. The wind would plunge the temperature, with the constant river mist making minimal comfort zones. With the obvious built in dangers associated with railroading, this was one rough and tumble place to work. Note the many lighters and other craft moored south of the yard.

The Erie, DL&W and EL Railroads

The Erie's tri set of electric float bridges were located between Piers 6 and 8. By the 1960's pier 6 would be gone, leaving a perimeter of pilings as a reminder of its past presence on the Jersey City Hudson River Waterfront. Note the Erie water tank above the float bridges. 1954

Jersey City was never known for being a deep water port. Most movements of cargo were accomplished with the use of Lighters and barges. All of the railroads on the waterfront did have piers set up for ocean going vessels and tried their best to keep them occupied. Direct ship to land transference of freight eliminated the need for other water bound craft knocking down the costs of labor considerably. This vessel is moored at the Lackawanna's pier 10. Note the trailer trucks on the elevated roadway leading into the third level of the Pier 10's warehouse. The sights one beheld in Jersey City were not only unique but never to be repeated again. 1954

Erie tug New York is parked at the end of Pier 4 with its roof mounted emblem. The Railway Express Agency utilized the pier for many years. To the left is the Erie passenger terminal and slips. Note the protective pilings alongside Pier 4's southern exposure. Even a slow moving ferry boat would have caused terrible damage to a structure resting on pilings. 1954

Overview Map of the Erie Railroad Facilities in Jersey City

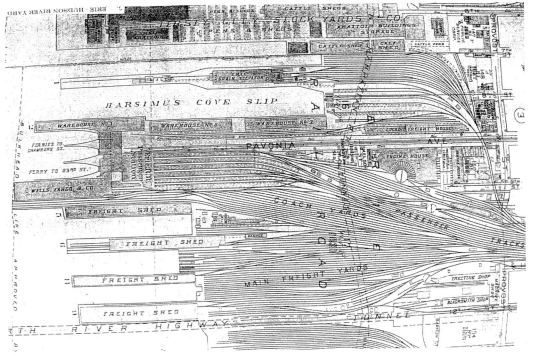

The Erie's ferry boat, Tuxedo is starting another run eastward laden with a pair of trucks peering out at Manhattan. In front of them are a few men braving the cold. I can recall the excitement I always felt when placing myself at the bow on a ferry boat crossing. Cutting thru the water as the opposing shore grew closer was always worth the discomfort of the elements. 1954

This Aerial photo shows the influence of the railroads and the surrounding industrial entities that populated the Jersey City waterfront. For over a hundred years much of the city's land was used for the creation or transportation of finished goods along with raw materials. The Erie Lackawanna Terminal yards made up for its abbreviated length with its considerable width. Strings of cars were limited, so multi tracks would be utilized to make up trains. The EL's three Float Bridges each have a car float moored but only the center one is loaded. At the left of the Float Bridges is the open expanse of river that not so long ago was the Erie Passenger Terminal. All that remains are the tracks leading to waters edge and a couple of signal towers. January 30, 1961

The Erie railroad began as the New York & Erie Railroad in 1832. In 1861 the name was shortened to the Erie. The line first reached Jersey City in 1848. In 1864 a ferry service across the Hudson River was purchased, initiating passenger operations to New York City. This route would last 92 years when the Erie moved passenger operations to the Lackawanna's Hoboken Terminal. The Erie merged with the Lackawanna Railroad on October 17, 1960. It would not take long for the Erie Lackawanna railroad to consolidate the bulk of its combined freight businesses onto the larger DL&W Hudson River spread.

The Delaware, Lackawanna & Western Railroad also was conceived in 1832 as the Liggetts Gap Railroad. The DL&W Railroad was chartered in 1850. The DL&W joined the Jersey City pack in 1868 with the purchase of the Morris & Erie Railroad. The Jersey City Freight business, combined with its Hoboken Passenger Rail and Ferry Terminal quickly, became one of the region's transportation winners.

The Erie Lackawanna merger created a railroad with 3,031 miles of track, 31,747 freight cars, 1,158 passenger cars, 695 diesel engines and 20,000 employees. 35,000 passengers rode 200 trains daily, half of the Hudson River area's total ridership. Ferry service came to an end in 1967 with long distance trains following in 1970. The EL would do its best to survive but the inherited expenses and an out of control overhead were too much of a deadly foe. By 1976 the EL would be gone. One day it was there, the next day it simply disappeared and became a memory.

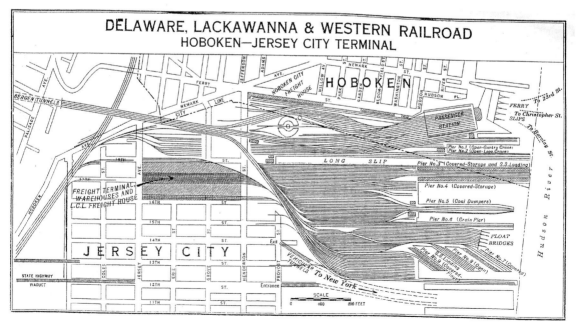

The Erie's warehouse just north of its triple float bridges covered the full surface of Pier 8. Hudson River piers like this one contained massive amounts of square footage. Back in the 1950's a lot of storage space was a necessity to take care of the business at hand. Rail and road freight was not computer timed and could not be relied on regularly, so it was only natural to have all the freight on hand. 1954

ERIE-LACKAWANNA RAILROAD - ANNUAL RAILROAD FREIGHT, JERSEY CITY WATERF

Year	Total Annual Freight	Local Freight	Tidewater Coal	Grain Lighterage	Merchandise Lighterage
1960	--	--	1,091,734	--	1,077,88
1959	3,087,469	1,095,696	910,499	--	1,071,17
1958	3,495,014	1,116,099	1,104,508	--	1,247,38
1957	4,262,645	1,490,973	1,079,002	--	1,690,29
1956	4,449,560	1,542,539	1,140,223	--	1,760,89
1955	4,063,541	1,637,146	882,043	--	1,527,15
1954	3,463,691	1,387,452	643,460	--	1,415,72
1953	3,537,383	1,375,581	649,970	--	1,488,13
1952	5,285,467	2,696,275	948,422	--	1,616,12
1951	3,860,894	1,299,878	946,150	--	1,583,71
1950	4,417,868	2,010,700	1,102,331	--	1,270,53
1949	4,357,912	1,531,486	1,010,413	--	1,665,36
1940	4,243,213	1,250,895	1,430,195	--	1,445,62
1939	3,705,817	609,948	1,711,012	--	1,261,55

Source: Port of New York Authority, Port Development Department

The Erie Lackawanna railroads presence on the Hudson River was noticeably lessening along with all the other lines by the 1960's. This aerial shot of the EL waterfront operation presents a picture dominated with a vacant expanse of land and river where recently a terminal and ferry station recently stood. The tug guiding the car float to a waiting slot at the Float Bridges will not have a problem finding room for the cars with the yard tracks mostly vacant. The only ground action is the concrete surfaced truck to the train yard area. This was still a labor intensive era when the outdoor exchanges of freight from one mode to another was a common process. Note the lines of parked autos right up to the piers edge. In only a few years employees of the waterfront railroads went from taking a train or a bus to work to driving a car to the job. Since the end of WWII millions went the way of the American dream. The new reality became a car in every garage. Before the war very few workers owned a house let alone a garage. Prosperity would initiate the freedom of upward mobility yet unknown to the bulk of the American people. With it would come the many changes in industries like railroading.

An Alco swither heads a New York, Susquahanna & Western Railroad local passenger train underneath the signal bridge located at the entrance to the Erie Railroad's passenger terminal in Jersey City. 1952

Behind the DL&W Pier 8 is the massive double track trestle that ran atop Grain Pier 6. This was another example of the diversity of Jersey City's waterfront infrastructure. Alongside the elevated wooden structure is the yard that led up to the float bridges. The Lackawanna's freight yards were basically all located in Jersey City.

Erie Lackawanna Jersey City Trackage in the 1960s

The Lackawanna had three piers that did not face directly east. In view are Piers 8 & 9, Pier 7 is not in this shot. This is where the Erie and Lackawanna properties met. The multi tracks at the right lead up to the DL&W's Transfer bridges. Beyond the freight cars was the DL&W's grain trestle. Running along pier 8's eastern side is a below water level double siding. This curiosity's integrity was accomplished by the purpose built retaining wall. The retaining wall itself was shielded from a stray lighter's hull by a tightly bound row of pilings. 1954

The Belt Line

Belt Line 13 looking south in the vicinity of Hoboken Ave. and the EL Monmouth Street Yard.

This view of the Belt Way approaching the EL's Monmouth Street Yard gives the impression of an openness not experienced in decades. 1960's

A Great Northern boxcar is part of a string of rolling stock atop the EL Bridge heading for the Bergen Arches. Under the EL line is Belt Line 13 which is also elevated. Traces of the EL line still remain near the Eastern entrance to the Bergen Arches in one of Jersey City's last non park wooded areas. 1960's

The multi track Erie Bridge crossing the Belt Way once carried traffic to the Bergen Arches. Many rail bridges were built in Jersey City and most were not single tracked. The Public Service Trolley Line ran along the right of way on the left. 1960's

The EL passenger main crosses the Belt Line where the tracks curve southward. The turnout to the left is the connecting track to the elevated EL line. 1960's

The Bergen Arches were in a state of neglect for many years as this photo reflects. Eventually the line was rebuilt to modern standards and is used modestly today.

Hoboken

DL&W's classification yard was just short of where Jersey City and Hoboken met. To the right is Hoboken with the EL passenger terminal, storage and maintenance tracks. The classification yard was of a short, wide design. This layout provided the capacity needed to store the large amount of rolling stock a multi tiered waterfront railroad business like the Erie Lackawanna demanded. A pair of Gantry Cranes run nearly the length of the Long Slip to lift the lumber in seemingly endless demand of the housing boom of the 1950's. The DL&W is moving plenty of this commodity this day, filling twin rows of gondolas that are lined up under the rolling cranes. The crated goods are piled high waiting for empty flat cars to haul them away. The coal hoppers will soon find their way up the coal piers trestle to be dumped into the hull of barges. Things were jumping at the DL&W yards during the summer of 1951.

The DL&W's Pier 3 warehouse was covered from one end to the other. The pier was also used as mooring for sea going vessels. At the bottom are Piers 7, 8 and 9. There are box cars on the piers themselves but the yard is clear of cars of any type. January 15, 1964

This overview of the EL yards and piers shows the freight and passenger trackage joining on the Hoboken side. The layout of the old DL&W caused freight traffic to veer southward once off the main line into the different yards. This is the reason for the short, very wide freight yard that dominated Jersey City's border with Hoboken for many decades. January 15, 1964

Right: Catenary dominates the scene at the western end of the EL's Hoboken Passenger Terminal Yard. With the Aldene Plan on the horizon, all of the Hudson River railroad's commuter traffic would be funneled into Hoboken's EL Terminal. Only the Hudson & Manhattan would remain in Jersey City. Today, Hoboken handles thousands of people heading into New York City making it an important part of the areas transportation system. 1960's **Below:** The EL's Terminal piers had dumpers to handle grain coal and other products. Twenty years earlier, during the height of WWII, hoppers were shoved up the ramps of both piers night and day to fill the hulls of impatient Liberty ships. In 1964 the pace has slackened but the action is the same, the goods are still headed to the river.

Right: A couple of EL supervisors are out on a very warm summer afternoon. Suit jackets draped over their shoulders, they head back to their desks withen the shade of the Hoboken Terminal shed. 1960's **Below:** The EL had a minor presence in Weehawken that was inherited with the merger. The 6 piers all appear to be very active in this 1961 photo. An abundance of rolling stock have cramped the curved tracks leading onto and into the piers. This would have been a welcome sight at any point along the Hudson River Waterfront.

Trackage Around the DL&W Dumper

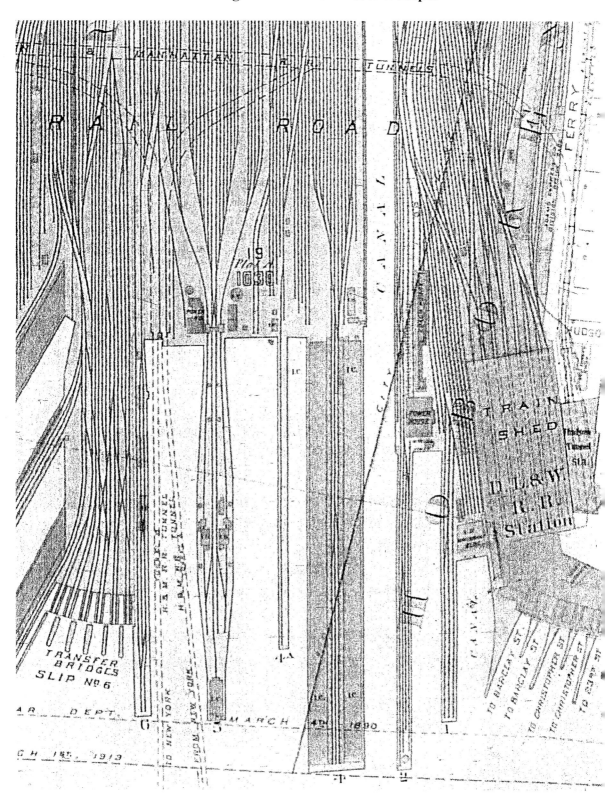